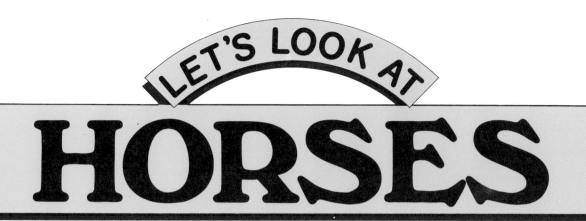

LET'S LOOK AT HORSES

Kenneth Quicke

Language Consultant
Diana Bentley
University of Reading

Artist
Wendy Meadway

Wayland

Let's Look At

Castles
Colours
Dinosaurs
Farming
Horses
Outer Space
The Seasons
Sunshine

First published in 1988 by
Wayland (Publishers) Ltd
61, Western Road, Hove
East Sussex, BN3 1JD, England

British Library Cataloguing in Publication Data

Quicke, Kenneth
  Let's look at horses. – (Let's look at).
  1. Horses – Juvenile literature
  I. Title
  636.1   SF302

ISBN 1–85210–224–1

Editor: Francesca Motisi

Phototypeset by Kalligraphics, Redhill, Surrey
Printed and bound by Casterman, S.A., Belgium

Words printed in **bold**
are explained
in the glossary.

Contents

What is a horse?

A horse is a mammal. But what is a mammal? Mammals are animals like cows, pigs, rabbits, dogs and cats. All female mammals produce milk to feed their babies and usually these babies are born live, not from eggs.

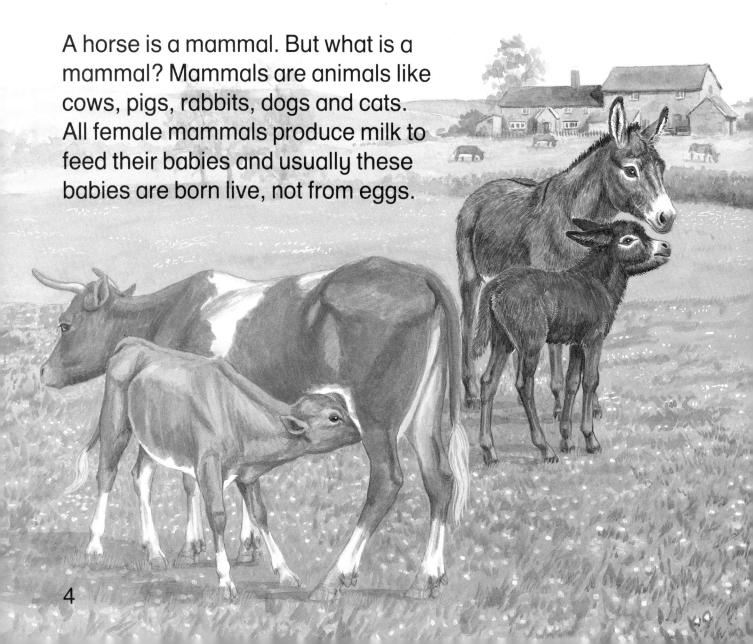

Horses today eat grass but the first horses ate leaves. Zebras, asses and donkeys also belong to the horse family. They all eat grass too and are called **grazers**.

5

The horse family

Horses usually live for about thirty years. Male horses are called stallions. Female horses are called mares.

A stallion

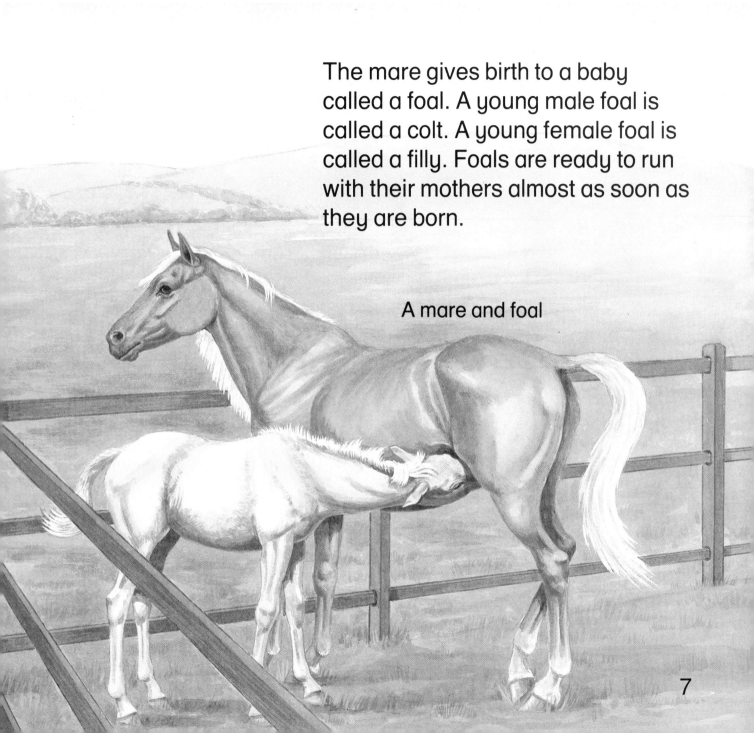

The mare gives birth to a baby called a foal. A young male foal is called a colt. A young female foal is called a filly. Foals are ready to run with their mothers almost as soon as they are born.

A mare and foal

Przewalski's horses

Many years ago a Russian **explorer** called Przewalski found a **herd** of **wild** horses in Mongolia.

A herd of Przewalski's Horses

The horses were given Przewalski's name. So they are called Przewalski's horses. Now they are very **rare** and most of them live in zoos.

Horse breeds round the world

Just as there are many different types of cats and dogs there are also many types of horses. These different types are called **breeds**. Today there are more than 200 breeds of horses throughout the world. How many breeds can you see here?

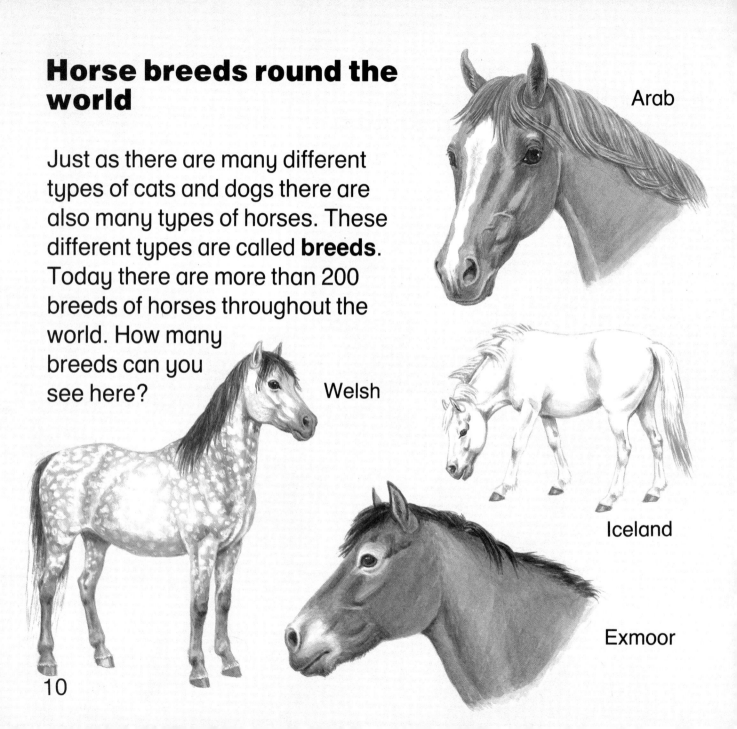

Arab

Welsh

Iceland

Exmoor

10

Australian Waler

Tennessee Walking Horse

Norwegian Fjord

Connemara

Ardennes

11

Horse colours

Bay

Horses come in many different colours. Gold-coloured horses are called Palaminos. Spotted horses are called Appaloosas. Look at some of the other different colours of the horses in these pictures.

Palamino

Appaloosa

Chestnut

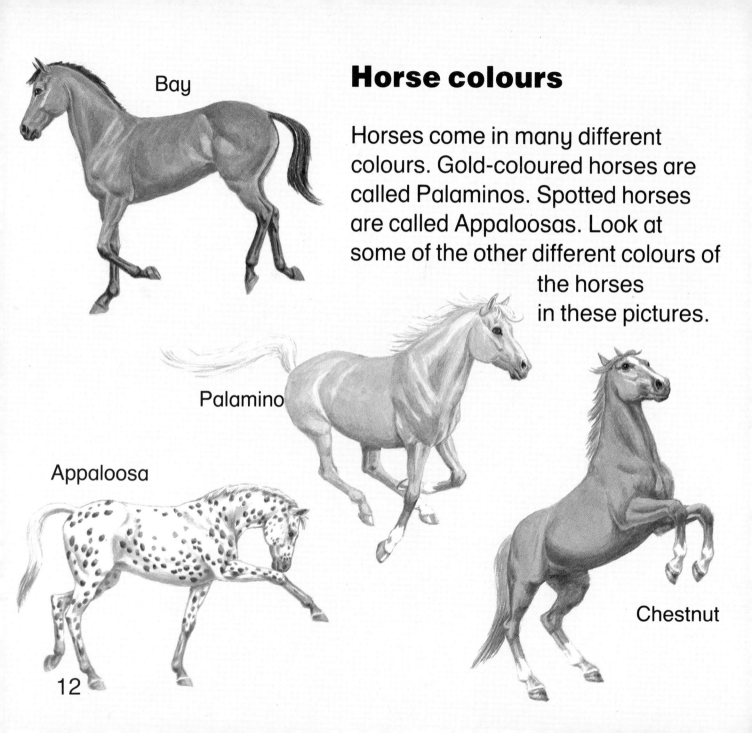

Dun

Roan

Black

Piebald

13

Working horses round the world

In some countries the police use horses in their work. The Canadian Mounted Police are called Mounties. The Mounties sometimes wear bright red uniforms.

A Canadian Mountie

Today most horses are used for riding but some horses are still used for work like delivering barrels of beer. Until about forty years ago milk was delivered by a cart pulled by a horse. These carts were called milk-floats.

Shire horses

Horses on the farm

Horses used to do all the heavy jobs on farms. Farmers trained the horses to pull a plough.
In summer the horses pulled the hay-carts. In the autumn the farmer and his horses worked long hours gathering the harvest. Today tractors make these jobs quicker.

A Percheron ploughing team

In some places horses are still used for farm work. This is because four legs can often get over land where the wheels of a tractor would slip and slide. In some countries it is cheaper to use horses than to buy machinery.

Ponies and cattle working in Northern Pakistan

Horses for transport

As long as 4,000 years ago horses in Egypt were used to pull carts. These carts were called **chariots**. People in Europe and North America travelled by stage-coach before there were cars and trains. Look at the stage-coach in this picture.

A stage-coach

Over 100 years ago families travelled across North America in wagons. Each family followed another family in a wagon. This line of wagons was called a wagon-train.

A wagon-train

Horses in battle

In the past people used horses to ride into battle. The soldiers who fought on horseback were called the cavalry.

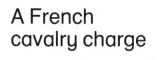

A French cavalry charge

Soldiers who fought on foot were called foot soldiers. When the cavalry rode into battle they **scattered** the foot soldiers.

21

Horses for hunting

People used to hunt animals for food. Often they did this on horseback. The native Americans used horses to hunt buffalo.

In Assyria 2,000 years ago people rode in chariots and hunted lions with bows and arrows. Sometimes the Assyrians rode on horses and hunted animals with swords.

Native Americans hunting bison

Horse cousins

There are other animals belonging to the horse family. The zebra is the most well-known relative of the horse. They live in herds on the African grasslands.

24

The mule, donkey and ass also belong to the horse family. The asses in Africa are related to donkeys. Donkeys are still used throughout the world to carry heavy loads.

A herd of zebra watched by two African asses

Horses for sport

People use horses for many different types of sport. One of these sports is racing. Another is show-jumping. People enter showjumping competitions to see whose horse can jump the best.

Showjumping

A rodeo

In North America cowboys and cowgirls enter competitions called rodeos. One famous rodeo event is trying to stay on a wild horse. These wild horses try to throw off their riders by jumping around. This jumping around movement is called bucking and so the horses are called bucking broncos.

Looking after horses

In the summer horses can be kept in fields. In the winter when the grass stops growing horses need extra food and somewhere to keep warm.

Horses used for riding or pulling carts on roads need to wear metal shoes to protect their feet. These metal shoes do not look like the shoes we wear! The person who puts these shoes on to the horses' feet is called a blacksmith.

A blacksmith at work

Glossary

Breeds Different sorts of the same animal.

Chariot A two-wheeled horse-drawn cart used in ancient Egypt, Greece and Rome.

Explorer Someone who travels to unknown places.

Grazers Animals that eat grass.

Herd A large group of animals living and feeding together.

Rare Not many left.

Scattered To go different ways.

Wild Animals that have not been tamed by people.

Books to read

A Day With A Riding Instructress by
    Pippa Cuckson and Tim Humphrey
    (Wayland 1982)
A guide to Horses and Ponies by
    Catherine Dell (Pan 1979)
The Blacksmith's House by Joy James
    (Black 1979)
The Vet by Nicky Daw (Black 1985)
Zebra by Mary Hoffman (Methuen 1985)
Zebras in the Wild by Cliff Moon
    (Wayland 1985)

Index